AF237644

When you change the way you look at things, the things you look at change.

Max Planck (1858-1947)
Founder of quantum physics, Nobel Prize 1918

Udo Brückmann

The Brueckmann-Method
Tangible ways
in fantasy worlds

Coaching

Bibliographic information from the German National Library:
The German National Library lists this publication in the German
National Bibliography; detailed bibliographic data are available on
the website *http://dnb.d-nb.de.*

Environmental notice:
This book was printed on chlorine- and acid-free paper.

Copyright © 2021 Udo Brückmann
Manufacture and publisher: BoD – Books on Demand, Norderstedt
Cover: Udo Brückmann
Printed in Germany

ISBN 978-3-7534-8291-0

Contents

Foreword

The Brueckmann-Method, which bears my name and is presented to the public for the first time, has a potential to sustainably enrich the coaching business.

In order to develop the method and write these lines, it took 35 years for me to deal with a wide variety of spiritual topics. Quantum physics and quantum healing have become more and more the focus of fascination.

Basically, however, it all started with a near-death experience a long time ago that literally kicked my life out of the orbit after an infection had been taken away. During this special situation between life and death, as a young person, I have not only been outside of my physical body for a certain time, I have also been able to observe this body very clearly from outside. And I cannot be what I have observed – according to the knowledge – because the observer is obviously something completely different from the physical body with which he is connected. If the connection had dissolved, so that I would have died, only my physical body would have died, my "experiential instrument". So our life, according to the reflection at that time, must involve much more complex matters than just the three dimensions of our material existence. Since then, I have dealt with the all-encompassing theme of human consciousness. This also includes the influential, yet incomprehensible subconscious as part of every personality.

One day I wondered, how it can be possible to use one's own dreams in such a way that, after waking up, one can remember exactly all the details in order to understand the messages from the dream world and thus from the subconscious, and to gain the corresponding insights from them. The answer is: Not at all. Each of us will always be just the dreamer, who does not remember his dreams or only remembers them a little. Everything melts away in fragments between your fingers and is simply gone again. Likewise, it makes no sense to reprogram or reorient the subconscious in an elaborate manner, if the results remain unsatisfactory. Even lucid dreaming or "clear dreams" – you dream and are aware that you dream – are insufficient for me, because the desired results are just random.

My coaching method, on the other hand, shows the user the possibility of bringing the mostly inaccessible dream world of our free fantasy, which largely affects the subconscious in sleep, into conscious reality in order to make it interactively experienceable there. Even more: The method is about getting into a higher consciousness and thus into a reality that is far superior to our three-dimensional existence.

So that this state of knowledge can be reliably achieved, elements from quantum healing are used, combined with a special way of "light breathing", with which you create your double, your "light twin". This process is an important process of my method which takes place in your imagination.

The requirement for this is that you should be a visual person, because the intensity of imagination does a large part of the success in working with the method. By the way it is of course possible to practice visualizations with appropriate exercises.

It is important to mention that the coaching sessions have nothing to do with role-playing games, where you assume a different identity to escape from your problems and worries. No. If this were the case, you would act merely as your ego, as your low-dimensional personality with its limiting rational mind and again with its subconscious, who wants to take control as usual.

By identifying with the figure you embody during the coaching session within a "fantasy world" you choose, you become this character yourself. For the duration of the coaching you are this individual figure, that has never existed before in the fantasy world.

You are "traveling" together with your "light twin", so that your subconscious is tricked and set aside. The method shows you, that you can open yourself to the awareness of higher dimensions, because you, like every other living being, are naturally an energy body in different stages of energetic compression. Otherwise, the effects of quantum healing would not be explained. So you are no longer identified with your ego or your I, but with your I AM. You learn to take spiritual responsibility for yourself, because for everything that happens to you in life, you alone bear the responsibility. And no one else on this planet.

The Brueckmann-Method wants to help you to discover your creative nature, comprehend it holistically and use it positively. Not in theory, but in practice – for a better life according to your very personal needs and standards.
I would like to explain larger contexts and put them in relation to one another.

After each chapter, you will find a short summary on an extra page to facilitate the practical work with this book.

As a coach and consultant, it is a great pleasure and an honor for me to support an active part of mental life and mental health.
Please also note that English is not my "mother tongue" or first language. So the translation from German wasn't that easy.

May the method serve the light and well-being of all people who understand the beauty of life.

Udo Brückmann, March 2021

"The Bueckmann-Method – Tangible ways in fantasy worlds" is legally protected by copyright and notarial certification.

Introduction

The Brueckmann-Method concerns not a classical meditation, it's much more like a mental accompaniment into the "fantasy world" which you determine yourself in your selection. More about this in the next chapter.

As an author of highly imaginative and fantasy stories and a many years' confrontation with consciousness and quantum healing it is my concern to unite these subject areas in my coaching. The free imagination is the highest creative force which is available to every person without limitation. If one activates and connects this power with the intuition, the inspiration, the internal voice or something from a "gut reaction", an all-embracing source of creativity and miracles opens which includes the answers to all questions and a lot that goes beyond this. Each person becomes a creator as a part of the universal whole. This can happen, as already mentioned, also in dreams, but only there operates the subconsciousness, so that the dreamt events can remain only one as a vague recollection and cause almost nothing in the reality. Or very little.

So my coaching method is about creating a conscious connection to stop focusing on the rational mind and the ego and finally direct it into the heart. This is the place and at the same time the metaphysical area, in which honest and "unfiltered" answers can be transmitted to you, including all the answers you don't really want to hear. That is exactly what it means, to take mental responsibility for yourself in order to step out of your own comfort zone. And this is not an easy walk or a fun experiment to consume, but a serious attempt to successfully resolve an energy blockade in order to return to the natural flow of life, to optimize the quality of life in several ways. The inner balance that is achieved in the end, is a balance between thoughts and feelings.

It's about attracting a higher consciousness. This higher consciousness knows no time and no space as it corresponds to human understanding. So you enter supposed new territory and act as a discoverer: whatever you will find in the end, it is yourself and will always be yourself. And this is the essence of your being which only has a small intersection with your human mirror image. At last, you will find that it is only a rediscovery, a lost memory.

Quantum physics happens outside of our causality, but plays with its probabilities which condense into our three-dimensional realities through perception. Cause and effect presuppose a linear time which is consistent with the principle of quantum physics and contradicts it at the same time.

If you try to understand all these things only from the rational mind, you will fail and stay on an open track with your experiential instrument "body".

Although you can understand the content of this little book with the help of your rational mind, I would still like to prepare you to refrain from doing so during the application of the method to open and entrust yourself to a higher force in higher dimensions. Hypnosis, suggestion or similiar things are not used here.

By the way, it does not matter which religion or spiritual direction you belong to, because my method has nothing to do with believing in something in the sense of a religious piety. Something that is somehow "outside" of you, how many organizations or power structures would like to pretend to you. On the contrary, it is all "inside" of you, because you not only connect with a higher consciousness, you are already an inseparable part of the highest consciousness, just like every other person. Whether you call this "God", "the Higher Self," "the universe", or anything else, is entirely up to you. This also corresponds to the holistic explanation model of quantum healing. The "faith" is the inner certainty that your own expectation will be fulfilled because you can check it yourself.

You do not have to throw your worldview overboard, but I urge you to broaden your spiritual horizon and loosen all too firmly anchored perspectives or change the point of view to become free of external boundaries which can ultimately lead to internal boundaries. This is always tailored to your individual consciousness, which moves within a mass consciousness, but is not depending on it.

What the majority thinks, feels and believes and thus decisively influences the reality around us does not have automatically a relate to your own beliefs. As an individual, you have not only a free imagination, but also a free will which no power of the world can take away from you. Only as your own sovereign you can awaken to yourself and unfold your creative potential. The task is not to receive superordinate structures as (controlled) devotees, but to act as yourself independently with the help of the free spirit. Once this freedom is compromised, you should question the structures. In your life you are the boss and not the intern.

For the application of my method, it is not absolutely necessary to be aware of the background information that are provided here. The functioning of the method is not impaired, but as a coach I am of course obliged to the reader and user to clarify all details. Also, to calm your rational mind, which may be in turmoil, because he thinks the basic ground under his feet will be pulled away. There is no cause for such concern.

The Brueckmann-Method is about knowingly learning about oneself. This can be the solution to a problem, overcoming an obstacle or the missing spark for an initial ignition.

As a coach and empathetic person, as a mediator and companion, I am the one who points to "open doors", to unexpected possibilities that become visible during the coaching. New perspectives can change your life positively in just one moment. Although I take you mentally on the experiential paths, you are and remain the main character in your individual story. You alone determine the way through your "fantasy world". Be open to surprises and unpredictable twists.

A negative event does not always have to be in the foreground. Likewise, positive circumstances, such as celebrity and social prestige as a permanent fulfillment of a public expectation, can completely put life out of balance. For example, I gained experience with actresses, actors and other cultural artists. Of course, I never mention names in public, because it is not just a service, but also a great trust that must always be respected. Trust affects every age and every social position, absolute discretion is guaranteed.

What I am not as a coach – and you should keep that in mind – is a medical-psychologically trained counsellor. Hence, with serious health problems, as for example the treatment of depressions, you should visit a suitable specialist. Attention: To make diagnoses or to give recommendations for medical therapies is not my job. Also I pursue no certain religion, political direction or ideology, only the human is in the central of my endeavors – as well as to use one's own universal creative power in the sense of the free spirit and to make it individually experienced.

Legal notice: My coaching is a trustful consulting activity as a service, a help for self-help. This activity, for which I assume no liability, is never to be equated with medical consultations with a specialist in the case of physical or mental diseases and illness of any kind. Again: In case of serious health problems or medical risks, please ask your doctor!

Sometimes patience and exercise are also required, because the desired results cannot be enforced.
Success and working with the method also depends on the extent to which you are willing to encounter yourself, to look deep inside yourself. But I can assure you: it's worth it.

Summary "Introduction":

- brief explanation of the Brueckmann-Method
- free fantasy as supreme creativity
- conscious connection with the fantasy world outside the subconscious
- connection to a higher consciousness
- release energy blockages
- conscious knowledge about oneself
- questioning your own view of the world
- exclude the rational mind and ego
- self-determination in the sense of free spirit and free will
- coaching as a trusting service
- Brueckmann-Method suitable for everyone
- discretion during execution
- outside religion, ideology or political direction
- no replacement for medical consultations
- no diagnoses or therapy recommendations

Legal notice: the coach assumes no liability whatsoever, in case of health problems please contact your doctor!

The seven fantasy worlds

The number 7 is not only a prime number, but also a very special number from the mysticism of various cultures and traditions. The magic number 7 represents the union between mind and matter, the 7 represents spiritual wisdom and inspiration. In Hinduism, according to the ancient assumption, the number 7 even opens the paths into the universe. There are "seven oceans", "seven wonders of the world", "seven dwarfs" or seven colors of the rainbow. And so for good reasons there are also seven fantasy worlds within the Brueckmann-Method. The 7 is the number of changes to the positive, which comes closest to the essence of the method.

Before the method can be started, make a selection: You decide personally and depending on your preference for the "fantasy world" in which you want to move interactively during the mental coaching.

In the following I will briefly introduce the seven worlds to you in terms of content, as they might be, but do not have to be. What you will experience is not predictable, because your free imagination is the actual "coach" behind the scenes.

You can choose from:

1. the space adventure

You are somewhere in the universe with your spaceship ... Perhaps you will discover strange planets or completely new forms of life? Or are you even the ambassador of a secret but very important mission?

2. the underwater world

Nobody has been in the deepest depths of the seas before you ... What about the silver underwater city and its enigmatic towers? Who will receive you there in your aqua-capsule? Is it a mermaid?

3. the time machine

Enter the desired year and the desired location, buckle up and press "Start" ... Where are you going? In your own childhood or maybe in the Middle Ages - or even in a distant future? Who do you meet during your journey?

4. the oasis in the desert
In the middle of the infinity of the yellow sand desert you are stranded in a lush oasis, in which there is a secret wishing fountain ... Which wishes are fulfilled there? Or do you move on with a caravan?

5. the mystical labyrinth
This labyrinth with its huge dimensions is already waiting for you to enter it ... Are you alone? Which beings will show you the right way to find the great dragon? What does he have to tell you?

6. the education to become a magician
As a sorcerer's apprentice, you face great challenges ... But can you really use the powers of magic? What will your final exam look like in this schooling? And what will you do in your world afterwards?

7. the tree of life in the rainforest
The community that you discover or in which you live, including the houses, is located on a huge tree ... Is it an existence in a green

paradise? Or do enemies even invade from outside against whom you have to defend yourself?

Make your choice according to your "gut feeling" and let your intuition guide you in advance of the coaching. Do not think too much about it in which of the seven worlds you would like to be on the move. Remain in the here and now. Choose the "fantasy world" that most appeals to you right in this moment. Approach playfully and with adventurousness to the method. Of course, it is even better if you are already clear about which individual question you have answered or which problem you would like to have solved.

This applies to all seven fantasy worlds: no limits are set to the imagination and the free spirit.

Summary "The seven fantasy worlds":

- make an intuitive selection:
- the space adventure
- the underwater world
- the time machine
- the oasis in the desert
- the mystical labyrinth
- the education to become a magician
- the tree of life in the rainforest
- There are no limits to the imagination and the free spirit.

What energy means

The word "energy", which comes from the ancient Greek language ("energeia"), means "acting force". There are various forms of energy such as electrical energy, magnetic energy, mechanical energy, chemical energy, heat energy and so on.

First special feature: the individual energy form can be converted into another form. For example, if a battery is used, chemical energy is converted into electrical energy. Everyone knows that from everyday life.

Second special feature: energy per se is not lost and therefore cannot be generated; in any case, it will only be converted.

All school books on physics contain the well-known sentence "The total energy of a closed system remains constant for all processes." This is a very amazing fact, which is strangely little noticed. Basically, it's a sensation. If the concept of energy is also applied to metaphysical areas, these are suddenly taken out of the mysterious corner of mysticism and untouchable dogma: What really happens when I die, for example? Obviously I leave my material body behind with death, but the energy released remains in a lawful way constant within the (expanded) system, because energy cannot be lost. Instead, it is transformed. What religion calls the "soul" is directly linked to the highest consciousness and consciousness is the actual bearer of life, outside of time and space.

The "human system" consists of a visible and an invisible sector and exists simultaneously in different dimensions – including our three-dimensional reality. The entry into the visible sector is the birth and exit from the same the death. When the incarnation (lat. "in carne," "going into the meat") is over, therefore, life does not end. Quite the reserve. The physical body is a temporary phenomenon as an experiential instrument, but what I really AM and don't HAVE is indestructible. Once this circumstance has been internalized, a strong sovereignty develops to view life out of a completely new ease and confidence. Terrible things like accidents or diseases can happen to my body under certain circumstances, but nothing can happen here on the "holo deck" (like in "Star Trek") of the material 3D-experiences, which preserves this body as a part of consciousness and manages it for a certain period of time. This means once again not the I or ego, but the I AM. The rational mind remains completely outside.

As a vivid picture for the "system human being" I choose the comparison with a mushroom: the "actual mushroom" is an invisible braid in the underground and not the visible "fruit body". And if you pick this fruit body, the mushroom braid is of course still present, even if you can't see it.

We ourselves – and without exception everything around us – are ultimately energy. Or in other words, subject matter is nothing more than differently densified energy with a low, high or higher level of consciousness. This also affects every drop of water, every mountain or piece of metal, every blade of grass, every tree and every animal. Even if the rational mind bursts its collar again, sooner or later he will not be able to avoid acknowledging the basics of his presence. For this, however, the famous view over the (three-dimensional) plate edge is necessary.

I find it interesting that the classical atomic model is still used and taught to explain the world around us and its existence. This is the 1911 Rutherford atomic model. The notion of particles called "atoms" ("atomos", "indivisible" in ancient Greek), which are constructed in such a way that solid electrons move around a solid nucleus of protons and neutrons, is still as predictable as the planets on their paths around the sun. Although the physicist Niels Bohr only two years after Ernest Rutherford expanded his attitude to include quantum physical properties – the probability of electrons staying and not their precisely determinable positioning – this fact is largely hidden in popular science. It has long been clear that atoms are not solid, indivisible particles. Rather, as already mentioned, these are energy compressions.

Instead of a solid structure, one could describe as a subject matter model an energetic mist or an accumulation of mists in which – comparable to galaxies in the universe –

differently pronounced energy accumulations exist or appear apparently randomly to the probability; the stay of the electrons in it is not constant and cannot be accurately measured.

This coincidence is triggered by the intensity of perception in the connection with consciousness. Subject matter means energy, consciousness IS. It could also BE without subject matter, but subject matter is not possible without consciousness.

Atoms are the building blocks of our material world. The fact that the atomic nucleus represents only 0.0000001 percent of the total atom is extremely exciting; the rest – and this is the unimaginably large majority of 99.9999999 percent – is scientifically regarded as a vacuum, i.e. "space with the main absence of matter". Transferred into a size comparison, this would be about as if a pin head were lying in the middle of an Olympic stadium. From a purely physical point of view, therefore, our entire material world, the foundation of our reality, consists largely of nothing! That's not necessarily a satisfactory insight, isn't it? Perhaps the presumed "empty space" within each atom denotes the "seam" between material and spiritual reality? As the smallest unit holographically intertwined and penetrated each other? A "blueprint" for our reality and for the "human system" involving consciousness?

Electricity acts in each atom (including all divisible units). One cannot say "an atom has electricity", because the term lies outside of physical matter. Electricity covers all phenomena of dormant or moving electric charges and the electrical and magnetic fields surrounding them. The electrons are the carriers of negative electricity, the protons are the carriers of positive electricity. An atom is electrically neutral at rest without movement, since the electric fields of electrons and protons are the same size – and cancel each other out. If an imbalance of the electric fields or a negative or positive excess of the amount of electricity prevails in the atoms, this is expressed in the form of a negative or positive charge (measured in Coulomb), while the neutrons have no charge. Artificially, one creates a positive electrical charge in the atom by peeling off, a negative charge by attaching electrons (positive and negative ionization). If electrons or ions flow in metallic, liquid or gaseous conductors, this is referred to as current caused by the voltage existing between two charge carriers (measured in volts). Electricity works when the electrical equilibrium is lifted. At the same time, the phenomenon of magnetism acts in each atom. The term means the property of all occurring substances to show a force effect in a magnetic field. The electrons provide the reason for this, because each electron behaves like a miniature magnet with a north and south pole, as it rotates around itself with its electric charge. Each magnetic body is again surrounded by a magnetic field. The planet Earth also has a magnetic field.

Each atom has an electromagnetic oscillation (measured in Hertz), which would therefore have to be inherent in the metaphysical ability of a resonance or attraction force, which leaves and extends the material range of measurable electromagnetism. The oscillation can be varied depending on the intensity and is also present in all "feedback" information processing systems. In the case of "higher dimensions," the term "higher vibration planes" is also used.

The perpetual flow of spiritual energy – ideas, inspirations, solutions, etc. – is associated with a single source. And that is the source of consciousness.

Summary "What energy means":

- Forms of energy can be converted into other forms of energy.
- Energy is not lost, but is always converted.
- Energy cannot be generated.
- the law of conservation of energy in physics
- the human system: life and death
- metaphysical contemplation, material and spiritual world
- awareness of consciousness
- difference between I and I AM
- subject matter as compressed energy with different levels of consciousness
- Subject matter is not possible without consciousness.
- the classic and extended atomic model
- scientifically explained vacuum inside atoms, "seam" to the spiritual world?
- atoms as "building blocks" of subject matter
- electromagnetic properties of atoms
- higher vibration levels

Notes for your safety

The headline may sound more dramatic than it is in practice, but failure to comply with the safety instructions might cause physical injury if you sit on a barstool, for example, during the coaching. Why?

The 2-Point-Method from quantum healing, which is used here, usually causes unexpected physical reactions, all depending on the complexity of your topic, problem or condition, you want to change positively. Many people tilt backwards or to the side. It is therefore important to be careful and, as a safety measure, to ensure that you sit in an armchair (with armrests) or on a sofa while the coaching is taking place, so that your body is cushioned well in the event of falling. You can also sit appropriately on your bed, but should choose your position so that as a calculable possibility you do not fall with your head against a bed post or a bed edge.

When the blocked energy dissolves inside you, it may also be that further physical reactions come to light, even in combination. This can be a deep breathing, a tremor, slight swinging or even violent rocking movements, sudden crying, smiling or loud laughter. Just allow the physical reactions and don't be frightened. These pass quickly again and are no cause for concern. Also it can be that physically in the outside nothing happens at all. This is not predictable and depends on the complexity of your issue. After all, you look not only in the mirror, but in the innermost core of your personality and illuminated themes, which have sometimes already existed only in the dark for many years. And now you press the light switch of consciousness. You return holistically to the flow of life, as if a sealed or clogged source is again shoveled and cleaned, which is finally released with the pressure accumulated behind it. The fact that this pressure is accompanied by a wide variety of reactions of the body is understandable and quite normal.

One can perhaps imagine that the different dimensions must only gradually align themselves with the changed state in mutual interaction, since the energy quality has also changed. So a long-term effect can be expected.

Once again the prerequisite: you are alone in a room and have found a quiet and undisturbed place. In the background no music should run (also no "meditation music"; certainly not with water ploughing, because then you probably have to go to the toilet). Computers, tablets, smartphones and televisions remain turned off. And your appointment calendar will get the red card. All outside influences have a break, same with partners, family members, children or pets.

Necessary toilet facilities have already been completed. It should be equally clear that you do not drink alcohol, take nicotine or drugs before or during the coaching. I have to mention it anyway.

Having a handkerchief and a glass of water nearby may be helpful. And can you have a snack? No, you can't. So quench your hunger before the coaching or sometime afterwards. I also advise against chewing gum or candy during the coaching.

You should not suffer from fatigue or jetlag, as

the coaching would of course make little sense if you fell asleep. (Besides, my fee would go up without you noticing...)

If you are wearing glasses, take off the glasses. Comfortable clothing such as jogging pants, thick socks and so on is recommended, but not absolutely necessary. But if the belt and shoes are pressing, then please change this circumstance.

The prerequisite in a sentence: It is quiet around you, you rest in yourself, you are secured by a backrest and feel comfortable.

Summary "Notes for your safety":

- The 2-Point-Method can cause unexpected physical reactions.
- Caution: initially there is the possibility to tilt suddenly backwards or to the side.
- coaching only secured by a padded backrest (armchair, sofa, bed)
- other possible reactions: detailed respiration, light or violent shivering, swaying, swinging, crying, smiling, laughting
- No need to worry: the reactions are an indication that blockades are loosening.
- You are alone in a quiet room.
- undisturbed and comfortable place to feel good
- comfortable clothing (take off glasses)
- no distractions
- no food or tobacco products during coaching, of course no drugs
- no fatigue, no jet lag
- may have a handkerchief and a glass of water nearby

Intention and goal

As a preparation for the coaching, you should know your own concerns very well and be clear about your topic, your problem or the situation you want to change in a positive way. Very clear.

That sounds simple, but it is often not. Strangely enough, many people do not know what they want at all, because the all-controlling everyday life sometimes leaves little clearance open to deal with themselves. Of course, this can also be an excuse, because it always seems uncomfortable to be asked to look inside yourself, where the hidden desires and secrets are buried. Fixed habits and today's consumer behavior are also pure distraction. Without a clear goal, however, you don't even have to start with the Brueckmann-Method.

Only you alone know your true intention. As a coach I can help you to formulate this intention so that it does not miss its effect. So please have a pen and paper ready!

You have two options: Either you keep your

goal as if in a personal treasure chest – during the entire coaching session – or you tell me right at the beginning which area of life you want to change. The decision has no influence on the outcome of the coaching, which in the end only affects your person and can only arise from your person. As a "mental companion", I'll be with you anyway. In addition, all confidential information is subject to confidentiality.

Much more important is the following decision. Question or support yourself: What exactly would you like to change? How strongly do you want the change in your life? Is this decision already determined as an irreconcilable intention or are you still playing with the sole thought of desire? If you only want to stay in your desire and have not made a decision, you will not change anything.

All possibilities in the different dimensions or vibration planes already exist at every moment. (See chapter "The matrix".) With the 2-Point-Method from the quantum healing, you resonate with the possibility of a reality to be realized, which corresponds to your intention and accordingly pours itself into a tangible form and thus becomes your reality. Your resonance field has thus adapted to the consciously changed state (energetically). So what is to do?

First of all, it is necessary to trick the subconscious again, because it does not know the meaning of "not" and "no". Both terms cannot be covered by the subconscious, so I would ask you to remove both words from the vocabulary of your intentions.

If I tell you: "Please do not think of a green elephant!", then of course you will think of it. The green elephant will appear in your imagination, he will not even ask you about it. So please do not use negations.

Your individual goal should always be formulated positively, consciously in the present form, not in the future. And certainly not as a possibility. Formulations such as "It would be nice if" or "I would like that" miss their effect. With such possibilities you are not even at the start. The reason for this is very simple: your consciousness only knows the present, because life takes place only in the here and now. In addition, you formulate your intention or goal as if you have already achieved it.

For example, if you have a problem falling asleep at night, your formulated intention is not "I want to be able to fall asleep immediately", but "I am preparing to follow my inner calm in a relaxed way" – or something like that. Another example: You are mobbed at work by a colleague. The intention is not "I wish my colleague to lose his job", but "Respect and balancing peace determine harmonious cooperation" or "May everything develop for the very best".

You immediately can tell the difference and that's what matters. Away from all compulsion and negation. Only positive produces positive. By this I mean the law of attraction "same attracts same things" and not "positive thinking", because only good thoughts don't do anything, they are part of the rational mind and the ego.

But you can consciously focus on your goal as clear as possible, because in your perceived idea the new reality has already arrived in your life full of joy and happiness: experience yourself within the positively changed situation or the intended subject area and perceive it with all your senses. Feel the change, smell, hear and taste it. By not only formulating your intention, but also seeing it as an irreconcilable decision as your goal of life, the law of attraction "same attracts the same thing" already works.

No one – including me as your coach – has claimed that it is easy to focus on deeper areas of one's personality between lunch, business meetings, housekeeping help and the late news, which may affect our mood and of which we are even very afraid.

Doubts are also completely normal. Allow the doubts to come and look at them. What do they want to tell you? Is the warning justified or does it block your path? Only you can know. But don't rate the doubts. Try to put them out of your mind.

Write your clear and unequivocal intention – in the present tense – on a sheet of paper and keep it during the coaching well obviously in your field of vision. As a coach I cannot see on the phone what you have written, so that you don't have to reveal what your goal is about. Of course, only if you have chosen this option. Otherwise I will help you as your coach with the right formulation.

My tip: In your imagination you can make from the sheet of paper a personal "treasure map" which you can take with you for orientation during the experiences in your "fantasy world". But even that is only your decision.

Summary "Intention and goal":

- Keep pen and paper ready.
- absolute clarity about your subject, your problem or the situation you want to change positively
- area of life or personal goal, either involving the coach or not
- What exactly do you want to change and how strong?
- The decision must be made so that your reality can resonate with it.
- Subconscious: delete words "not" and "no".
- formulate individual intention in the present form, positive and unambiguous (no form of possibility), namely in writing
- Only positive effects positive (law of attraction).
- Experience the goal with all your senses and feel as if it had already been achieved.
- allow all possible doubts, not evaluate them
- intention and personal goal as a possible "treasure map" for the "fantasy world"

About the breath and the light-twin

The breath means the amount of air that is moved during human breathing as a vital and life-sustaining action. On average, humans breathe about 20,000 times a day, which corresponds to a volume of twelve cubic meters of air. This amazing performance happens automatically as a reflex, without our intervention or willful effort. It just happens without you being really aware of it. After all, you've been breathing all your life. If you do not do it anymore, you have already left your physical body.

In Indian Pranayama Yoga, for example, breathing techniques are used to connect body and mind. It's the same in the Brueckmann-Method.

Breathing consists of two processes that, like the "yin and yang" – two opposing forces that partly contain each other – are irrevocably linked to each other: inhalation and exhalation. One is not possible without the other.

Breathing is used for internal cleaning,

because a large proportion of pollutants are excreted through the breath.

In yoga and jogging, it is recommended to inhale through the nose and exhale through the mouth. This makes better use of the potential of breathing; the circulation is stimulated, the heart beats stronger, the muscles come in momentum. This form of breathing should also be maintained during the coaching. Although it does not always succeed, since one simply forgets to keep the focus on the breath constantly, especially since at the same time the formulated declaration of intent is subject to a constant presence. But that's not a problem. It's enough if I remind you, as a coach, that you breathe in through your nose and out through your mouth when you create your "light-twin". At the same time, the abdomen expands during inhalation and curves as it goes back towards the spine while exhaling. This is important to explain the function of the solar plexus in relation to the 2-Point-Method. More about this in the chapter on quantum healing.

All body and brain cells are supplied with vital

oxygen while breathing and gas exchange in the lungs releases carbon dioxide. The respiratory center, which controls the breathing process, is located in the prolonged marrow of the brainstem as part of the central nervous system. So-called chemoreceptors are also involved.

Your lungs – protected by the thorax – are in constant exchange with your head. So far as the occurrence in the physical body. But what happens in the metaphysical, non-material sector?

Interestingly, unlike all other functions of the vegetative nervous system, breathing is deliberately controllable, that is, we can consciously put our decision into action to breathe slower, faster or deeper. Conscious breathing also generates relaxation and well-being.

You can also consciously connect breathing to your imagination: while you inhale, you imagine, for example, that you have already reached a specific goal or have positively changed an intention. And during exhalation, imagine yourself how to remove the corresponding unwanted goal and carry it out of yourself. This technique does not occur in the Brueckmann-Method. But I want to show you that conscious breathing has a key function of attracting to a higher level of consciousness.

With the breathing technique that is used during the coaching, you create – as I said – your own light-twin, your exact and brightly glowing double. In your imagination, let your light body emerge or arise from your spine. With each breath, your light-twin gets a little bigger and gains volume as if you were inflating a balloon. Once your light double has reached the exact size of your physical body, its "birth" is complete. It's not about communicating with your twin or even getting some advice or something like this. The luminous double remains completely silent. It is also not a "guardian angel" and certainly not your "split personality". Its only function is to constantly look over your shoulder during your fantasy journey, with everything that happens to you. Why?

The light-twin occupies a position from which

it observes you constantly and without judgment. With that, it is and remains in the perception like a camera, it leaves nothing and adds nothing. It thinks about nothing, it merely perceives the adventures you experience during coaching. Further nothing. By making it a symbol, a lighthearted embodiment, to end the prevailing identification with the I, the ego and the rational mind is guaranteed. The purpose of creating the light-twin is to trick yourself, because what you see with your twin's eyes cannot be you. (Similar to what I experienced in my near death experience.) In this way, it is possible to direct the focus, along with your intended goal, to the awareness, to your I AM and to maintain it for the duration of the mental coaching. This is the only way to get the answers you are looking for in a higher dimension, consciousness or vibration plane. The breath is only a means to an end and is not at the center of what is happening.

Summary "About the breath and the light-twin":

- meaning of breathing for the physical body
- breathing during coaching:: inhaling through the nose and exhaling through the mouth
- conscious breathing for the metaphysical sector as a gateway to a higher consciousness
- conscious breathing generates relaxation and well-being
- combining conscious breathing with imagination: creating your light-twin from your spine
- The light-twin remains completely in the perception, it does not communicate with you, it looks over your shoulder during the fantasy journey and watches the experiences without judgement like a camera.
- The identification with the I is terminated, because what you observe as your twin cannot be you.
- With your intention and objective, the focus is thus directed to your I AM, to a higher consciousness.

Quantum physics and quantum healing

The assumption that quantum healing is a direct development from quantum physics is wrong. The quantum theory of Max Planck from 1900 is considered to be the basis for quantum physics, radiation (or vibration) and subject matter can only exchange a certain and not arbitrary amount of energy, these energy units are called "quantum" (from Latin "quantum", "how much" or "how large"). Energy is not lost, but it is not just left somewhere. Quantum physics, which deals with the laws in atomic and subatomic fields or areas, is a scientific discipline based on complicated calculations. In my metaphysical understanding, however, quantum physics – consisting of quantum mechanics and quantum field theory – leads far beyond classical science, even if it is considered unserious by many of its present representatives. No wonder, because they use only the means of the rational mind, although the scientific results reveal the opposite for over 100 years. It's like if you had to explain to a circle what a bullet is. You could make countless attempts and would fail. The circle could only be helped on the path of knowledge by a "quantum leap". From a circle perspective, this would be comparable to a very large jump in consciousness.

Quantum effects have long since arrived in our everyday lives. They play an important role, for example, in lasers, transistors or in electron microscopy. Many quantum physicists, however, only focus on lighting and information technology with their research – rather than on consciousness technology. Taking into account all aspects of quantum physics is not possible within the scope of this small book. (For "quantum field theory", see chapter "The matrix".)

The probability already mentioned in the chapter "What energy means" refers in quantum physics to the probable residence of a particle within a physically assumed space, such as an electron within an atom.

According to Werner Heisenberg (Nobel Prize for Physics 1932), the so-called "uncertainty principle" or the indeterminacy principle states in quantum mechanics that two measurable properties of a particle cannot be measured arbitrarily accurately at the same time. The situation of the particle or of the system in which it moves is subject to a wave function. A particle can appear as a particle and as a wave at the same time or only as a particle and only as a wave.

The most important example of a physical wave is the electromagnetic wave as a combination of electric and magnetic fields; as "obstetrician" the wave function of light (photons or light quanta) acts. The interaction of electromagnetic waves with matter refers to their specific frequency – or vibration.

Light waves act like particles and particles act like waves. The so-called "wave-particle dualism" means that subject matter can reach from A to B without moving through the intermediate space (quantum tunnel).

The wave function is described in quantum mechanics by the so-called Schrödinger equation, which, however, cannot be derived exactly mathematically. Erwin Schrödinger (Nobel Prize in Physics 1933) conveys in the equation named after him the probability of detecting particles in a certain physical space. The wave function contained therein is decisive for the propagation of the particles. When a particle moves through the physical space, however, its energy quantity does not change. In other words, the law of energy conservation applies, energy cannot be lost.

Within the system, I believe that energy adaption is happening, but why?

Erwin Schrödinger himself provides the answer in his famous thought experiment "Schrödinger's Cat": Imagine a cat in a closed and invisible box. It also contains a poison capsule whose decay is controlled by a radioactive atom. A completely random process. If the atomic nucleus disintegrates, radioactivity and thus the deadly poison is released. The question now is: what condition is the cat in? It is not possible to determine exactly whether the cat is still alive at a certain time (or measuring point) or is already dead. The duration of existence for a single atom cannot be exactly determined. According to quantum theory, the atom is in a situation or state of "superimposition", its state consists of two states simultaneously, already decay and not yet decay. Accordingly, the cat in the unopened box would also have to be in this state or in two states, simultaneously dead and alive. Only by an observer from outside, who finally opens the box, the final state of the cat is decided. And not before.

The existence of simultaneous states is also called "entanglement" in quantum physics, which very much contradicts classical physics. In a quantum physical system, a comprehensible overall state prevails, while a subsystem or several subsystems do not follow this overall state, since they assume their own state. The entanglement within the system is terminated as soon as one of the subsystems is fixed to a specific state of the system. The overall system is therefore variable and dependent on its subsystems. It is not predictable, but subject to all given possibilities of realities.

Two particles, which are intertwined but are located in two different places, are "spiritually connected", according to the correct physical term. If only one particle is observed, the state of the other particle is thus automatically determined, no matter how far apart both particles are spatially. (In 1997, Anton Zeilinger was able to experimentally prove a "teleportation" for the first time.)

Conclusion also in the case of "Schrödinger's Cat": the observer not only observes, he shapes the reality by observing it. He thus becomes the creator of his reality. The probability has been overcome.

And it is only in this way that an energy adaption of the observer and the observed thing becomes effective. This would be metaphysically equivalent to an overall quantum system, namely in its basic state of "zero-point energy". This is where the interface lies, in order to tap into a higher consciousness and make it available with the alignment to the same. Outside of thought, rational mind and ego. With conscious perception.

The "double gap experiment": If one shoots in an experiment set-up a single electron at a wall with two narrow, parallel and commensurate along columns, one would expect that one can prove the electron then either behind the left one or the right slit. Really, nevertheless, it is in such a way that the electron has passed both columns what can be proved on account of the illustrated pattern (interference pattern). Then even this still functions if one of both columns is only opened, after (!) the electron has flown towards the wall. It has moved, nevertheless, by both slits, although one has been obstructed of it. The unsolved question still remains, why the deliberate observer is not necessary in reation to the "double gap experiment" at all to achieve the present result. Consciousness itself could have much more unknown aspects.

The causality principle of our three-dimensional reality, the principle of cause and effect in relation to a linear time, does not occur in quantum physics under certain circumstances. Or does it? Life only takes place in the here and now. This now is shiftable on the quantum timeline: it would be able to set a cause where the effects have already occurred (past) and where there have been no effects (future), namely by means of an energy adjustment. Infinitely many possibilities of realities exist in parallel. How many of them are activated is decided by the perceiver or the one who taps the (higher) consciousness at the right moment. Whether time travel is really possible in our reality is only mathematically explored – as an extreme bending of rotating "black holes" in space. Attention: "antimatter" is also subject to consciousness.

The structure of the universe, research suggests, is most likely holographic, meaning that it consists of information in addition to subject matter and energy. Each part of the overall system carries all available information, each part again contains itself – on the basis of a wave function. Light as electromagnetic radiation or vibration leaves interference patterns (superposition).

Whether this is also the case in darkness, I leave as a question in the holographic space. There is no light in duality without darkness, but if you turn only to the bright side and entrust yourself, your creative potential will unfold to the full. Otherwise not. Darkness comes predominantly from the outside, but the light is already in you. Let it shine, because "the same thing attracts the same thing".

The first formulation of the term "quantum healing" goes back to the popular Indian-American physician and author Dr. Deepak Chopra, who recognized parallels between quantum physics, medicine and spirituality in the 1980s. New York's Time Magazine ranks him among the one hundred outstanding minds of the 20th century. The 2-Point-Method from quantum healing is not a new invention, but goes back to traditional Chinese medicine. (Acupuncture, for example, also works with the release of energetic blockages.) Everything that modern Western medicine cannot explain is gladly dismissed as a "placebo effect". When one firmly believes in effectiveness, this effectiveness is activated in reality. That's wonderful. Faith moves mountains! The result here has nothing to do with the "faith" in the religious sense of deep piety, but in turn only with the (unconscious) application of a quantum physical effect. How to name it doesn't matter. Faith is an excellent instrument for putting ideas into practice in a spiritual way. Everything that is outside your faith boundary cannot be realized. For example, if you say, "I firmly believe that I am a millionaire by tonight", I would like to emphasize that you are outside your faith boundary. The Brueckmann-Method is not about manifesting something directly, but about pointing out a way that answers the question from a particular subject area or provides an impulse, an image, an idea or a "flash of mind", which is to be done in order to consciously and not undercut the (clearly formulated) goal by dissolving an energetic blockade.

Quantum healing, like quantum physics, is an energy adaption whose process has already been described here. In quantum healing, a higher consciousness is tapped and made available. The energy adjustment takes place automatically. The keyword is "zero-point energy", whereby of course the purely physical explanation of the quantum vacuum cannot be meant. The zero point describes a "magical moment" that opens the gate between human being and higher consciousness in a mutual energy exchange and makes it permeable. Intuition, inspiration, the "gut feeling" or the inner voice take the lead. The desired information in response to a question about a specific area of life can be retrieved by means of perception. This is done either in words or in metaphors and images, which are usually shown directly to the questioner. But it can also happen after the coaching, so that the desired answer is subsequently "delivered". Compulsive wanting, however, blocks the result, because then you act out of the ego, out of your I – and not out of your I AM. You will notice this when you lose ease and playfulness. So that this does not happen, the Brueckmann-Method is based on different fantasy stories in which you can deliberately dive into an adventure world. The more you focus on a playful lightness and openness, the better the method works. Once again: It's not about a concept that you can impose on yourself in the outside. You are the main character in your story and only you bear the responsibility for yourself.

Quantum healing is an activation of self-healing powers, a help to self-help. All themes of life are addressed. The result always means a positive change, a walkable path for the better. Disharmonies are balanced in a holistic way, not only on the three-dimensional plane of the material body. As with the principle of quantum physics, the positive change of one level affects all other levels, so that in other words all further dimensions (on the path to the highest consciousness) are affected by it. It is interesting that there can also be positive changes in other areas of life, which have not been mentioned at all. For the released energy there is no limit, it simply flows to how and where it is needed to restore balance and harmony. However, what exactly happens in quantum healing cannot be formulated. This little book is of course only an attempt to explain the given and very complex circumstances with the rational mind, but not only. It is the intention of the author to perhaps even understand the phenomena described with your feelings of what quantum effects mean for consciousness.

The classic 2-Point-Method works continuously with the hands, the Brueckmann-Method works only at the beginning with them.

Although the hands act as measuring instruments, the 2-Point-Method usually attaches importance to individually finding the two points somewhere on the body on which the hands are to rest in an extra process. A distinction is made between the "topic point" and the "correspondence point". The two points are to be traced by emotionally trying out, which in my view can become a very "rational minded" way. After all, it is about consciousness – and finding the two points is not decisive. Where they are located exactly on the physical body is basically no matter. However, they have turned out to be a solid tool, so that the Brueckmann-Method also makes use of the two points. However, here the two points are fixed on two specific body regions. This is not a means of restriction, but of facilitated application, since it makes little energy sense to locate the points, for example, on the right large toe and the left ear lobe. (But should this or any other freely chosen variant suit you more, then just take it.)

During the coaching, the user's hands are ideally located at the beginning on two of the main human energy centers: This is the thorax area with the heart and the abdominal area with the solar plexus.

The heart not only has the function of maintaining the viability of the body by guaranteeing a stable and regular circulation, it also has a measurable electromagnetic energy field of two to three meters in diameter – around the heart. This amazing energy field is much larger and about 5000 times stronger than that of the brain. Nevertheless, traditionally the rational mind still serves as the main instrument of knowledge.

The energetic heart is the place where the highest consciousness can be made experiential. It is the place of love. The other two of the trinity are joy and gratitude.

If you feel and perceive something very positive with your heart, then love, joy and gratitude are the three companions.

The solar plexus or the "solar braid" is the area where, for example, the "butterflies" are when you are in love. The solar plexus (derived from Latin language, "sol" = "sun", "plexus" = "braid") is located under the diaphragm on the aorta, the main artery, as a lying braid or mesh of fibres of the vegetative nervous system, from which all the viscera of the upper abdominal cavity are supplied with nerves. In the physical body, the solar plexus is an autonomous nerve mesh in the upper abdomen, just above the abdominal cord. The strong electromagnetic field can also be measured. The nerves coming from the abdominal organs pass through the chest area high to the brain and vice versa. A targeted blow to the solar plexus can lead to nausea, dizziness or even unconsciousness.

Energy-wise, the solar plexus is the place of intuition, of inspiration and of course of "gut feeling", as the word says. The "inner voice" also corresponds to the solar braid, so as not to come into contact with judging thoughts from the rational mind. With the solar plexus, the sentient side of a human being is in the foreground and not the rational one.

In this practically applied 2-Point-Method from quantum healing, the heart and abdomen are consciously resonated, although the connection already exists purely physically.

One hand is responsible for the chest and therefore for the heart, the other hand for the abdomen and thus for the solar plexus. Which of the two hands – whether now the left or right – takes over the respective task, remains entirely reserved for you. Let the intuition decide spontaneously.

Note: The hand for the thorax area lies in the middle of the same and not directly on the heart. This is because otherwise you would focus on your own heartbeat. But that's not what the method is about.

Conclusion: Quantum healing has nothing to do with mysticism. It is an energy work with the help of consciousness. And why does quantum healing work? You for yourself consist to one hundred percent of energy. You are an energy being that has "condensed" for the purpose of human-earthly experiences – by means of your experiential instrument "physical body". (You only borrowed it here and have to hand it back to the dressing room later.) This in turn has the purpose of making consciousness perceptible as such, because you are consciousness or an inseparable part of it.

Is there a phenomenon that could prevent you from experiencing yourself as a conscious creator? Yes, this phenomenon is unfortunately very common: it is the counterpart to the highest energy form of love – and that is fear. It is based on ignorance, specification of false facts and manipulation. Your energy centres – of which there are seven in total – are covered and considerably restricted. Their "total vibration" is at a very low level. Fear is a control mechanism you don't need. No matter where the fear comes from, look at it and embrace it. This is the only way to give fear the chance to dissolve and disappear from your life. It's the same with grief.

This is the background information in order to start with the Brueckmann-Method: Don't think about any quantum effects, but just let them happen. Stay calm and relaxed without building too much pressure in the expectations, so you will have the best prerequisites to learn everything about yourself.

Summary "Quantum physics and quantum healing":

- Max Planck as founder of quantum physics
- concept of "probability": according to Heisenberg, particles can occur simultaneously as particles and waves (entanglement), Schrödinger equation
- thought experiment "Schrödinger's Cat"
- the human being is the conscious creator and guide of his reality, namely in the alignment of energy in reaching the "zero-point energy" in a higher consciousness, perception is determined by a possibility of reality.
- "double gap experiment," open questions
- holographic structure of the universe
- The 2-Point-Method from quantum healing goes back to traditional Chinese medicine.
- positive changes at all dimensions levels, quantum healing as energy work
- Brueckmann-Method: determining the two energy points on the chest area/heart and solar plexus, explaining these two physical areas and energy fields

Synchronize your hands

Before I explain my coaching method in detail in practice in the next chapter, there is still a small exercise to be completed, which is of great importance for the purpose of preparation: In the 2-Point-Method from quantum healing – as just explained – both hands are used, which represent the entire physical body.

The left hand represents the left half of the body, for which the right half of the brain is responsible. The right hand represents the right half of the body, so that the left half of the brain is increasingly used. To this end, one should know that the left brain is responsible for thinking with the help of the rational mind – logic, analysis, complex information, language – while the right brain is responsible for the feelings, that is, also for the imagination, fantasy, for everything playful, for ideas and "mental flashes".

The division of tasks of both brain halves is also called the "hemisphere model". Modern Western science now considers this model obsolete. Nevertheless: Transferring to the bits of a computer, the smallest electronic memory unit and unit of measurement for the information content, we have the following results: The left "rational" half of the brain can process a maximum of 40 to 50 bits at once, with the right "emotional" half of the brain it is – hold on – 10 to 11 billion bits at a time. Whether there will soon be a computer that can record it with the performance of your right brain half remains questionable.

For example, if the right half of the brain is affected in an accident, the physical consequences are particularly pronounced on the left half of the body – and vice versa. The body is thus controlled in two halves. That's a fact.

This "cross-over function" is dissolved during the application of the 2-Point-Method, that is, synchronization of the two brain halves takes place to a certain extent at the same time. Or a little more cautiously: In the head a certain communication between the neurons or nerve cells occurs. To assume complete synchronization of the brain seems a little exaggerated. Nevertheless, the 2-Point-Method provides a possibility for the mutual influence of both brain halves.

Exercise: Sit comfortably, relax and breathe evenly.

Slowly merge your two outstretched hands in front of the thorax area as if they were two magnets. The palms, fingers and thumbs approach each other without touching each other, because they gently repel each other.

Move your hands further apart and repeat the approach process several times. Vary the distance between the "magnetic" hands. Do not forget to breathe evenly.

Afterwards, focus on the palm of one of your hands. Then focus on the palm of the other one.

Now you perceive both palms simultaneously and observe the physical changes. This can be a tingling, a pulling or even heat. When you perceive a uniformity – a synchronization – you can expand the aspect of imagination when your eyes are closed:

In addition, go deeper into the imagination

and imagine that a "divider", "partition wall" or "curtain" opens between your two brain halves in order to enable the mutual exchange of energy between both halves even better. In any case, you support the entire brain performance and are in the holistic.

That's all. Now you are prepared for the Brueckmann-Method in practice.

Summary "Synchronize your hands":

- both hands represent the whole physical body
- the right hand stands for right body half, the left hemisphere is responsible (thinking: logic, analytics, complicated connections)
- the left hand stands for left body half, the right hemisphere is responsible (feelings: inspiration, imagination, fantasy), considerable achievement capacity
- By the synchronisation of the hands a synchronisation of both hemispheres also happens in a certain magnitude.
- practise for the preparation on the 2-point method: Both hands in front of the chest perceive as magnets and vary playfully the distances. Focus on the perception first only upon a palm, then only on the other, finally, on both at the same time, observe physical reaction.
- additional imagination: energy exchange between both hemispheres

The method in practice

Everything I talk about with a client before, during and after coaching remains strictly confidential among us. That is a matter of course, but I would like to mention it again. If you have chosen to inform me of your subject area, intention and goal, I make notes during the coaching session which I use afterwards to analyse the outcomes of the process. At the same time this is a reminder for you of your experiences in the "fantasy world". There is no tape recording or something like this.

The Brueckmann-Method is my offer of an applied life aid, which combines elements from quantum healing, breathing technique and imagination with the free fantasy, in order to reach a higher consciousness. For me personally, it is therefore very important that you know the legal reference to my work. Before we can begin the coaching, you have taken note of the legal notice, which I repeat again for this purpose at this point.

Legal notice: My coaching is a trustful

consulting activity as a service, a help for self-help. This activity, for which I assume no liability, is never to be equated with medical consultations with a specialist in the case of physical or mental diseases and illness of any kind. Again: In case of serious health problems or medical risks, please ask your doctor!

You have chosen one of the "seven fantasy worlds" for yourself, in which you want to move interactively during the coaching under guidance. You know the subject to be changed. Your intention and goal is formulated with positive words in the present form and is on a described note in your visual area. You can also carry this sheet of paper as an "imaginary treasure map" during the coaching. You have also read the chapter "Notes for your safety" in this book. The most important thing is that you are secured by a backrest and, if necessary, armrests if you initially tilt backwards or sideways as a physical reaction when energetic blockages come loose. In other words, you sit in a well-upholstered armchair, on a sofa or on your bed. (Or just in front of a wall if you're sitting on the floor on a carpet.) You are alone in a room and in a quiet environment, which should be the first basis for the coaching. Disturbing sounds in the background must be avoided. As well as anything that distracts. The silence serves previously to relax and then concentrate attention on the coaching.

It can happen – as I said – that you start to fluctuate, shake, cry or laugh. Or nothing happens physically. This is not predictable, individually different and depends on the spectrum of your topic or the situation you want to change positively.

Nevertheless, you should be prepared for all eventualities, because the physical reactions are a parameter that the intended changes are ready to enter into your life by releasing the blockages or at least showing that they are present in your subject area. There is no reason for concern about physical reactions. Having a handkerchief and a glass of water nearby can definitely not hurt. And the quiet place you have chosen for yourself should remain an undisturbed and comfortable place for the complete duration of the coaching. Including your clothes.

The Brueckmann-Method also works by the way in lying down, so this is my personal experience. Although there is a possibility that you will fall asleep during the coaching. In the imagination, you are in your "fantasy world" anyway most of the time standing, walking or running, whether you control your "avatar" now sitting or lying down. This is your personal decision, depending on your preference. I would still recommend the coaching while sitting. You'll see the reason when it comes to creating your "light-twin".

Are you ready? Then we can now move towards the "fantasy world" you have chosen. As a coach, I will accompany you into this world. The implementation of the Brueckmann-Method usually happens on the phone. You therefore need a corresponding device with a hands-free function or with headphones in order to have both hands free. The telephone version is well suited for focusing on yourself. But a personal coaching meeting is also possible.

Your intention is clear and you have the goal of your desired theme clearly in mind. If this is not yet the case, ask yourself which situation or goal you want to reach at the end. What is the ideal result for you to be completely satisfied? Imagine every detail as accurately as possible and experience this ideal situation as if it is already a part of your reality. Feel yourself into this new reality. Do not question the situation or the goal with the rational mind, because the mind immediately makes a judgment about it – mostly in the form of a limitation. However, we consciously enter a fantasy world where there are no such boundaries.

At the latest, you should have made the decision as to whether you want to keep your intention and goal to yourself – or to tell me as your coach which topic you want to change positively. Your decision has no influence on the outcome of the the coaching.

Trust yourself above all, and that your concern, your problem or your intention will develop and change in the best way that is possible at all. Leave the work to the quantum effects, your intuition and imagination, and hand everything over to a higher consciousness once you have arrived in the "zero-point energy". You cannot grasp that with your mind, but you will perceive the right moment. Just when it's done. Trust in your feeling. In case your rational mind speaks up, then make it clear that doubts and critical comments are not needed. Be nice to your rational mind, but don't let it guide you. When your mind is talking too much, show him the red card to leave the field.

Exchange your everyday life with the "fantasy world" you have chosen. Gradually, everyday life around you disappears. Nevertheless, pay attention to possible physical reactions and to the fact that in the case of the case you are picked up soft and well padded.

You sit straight, upright and leaning – and close your eyes. You breathe calmly and evenly without initially paying closer attention to the breath. Focus on the topic or situation that you want to change positively if you don't already have.

Read and internalize the lines of your intention

either mute in thought or speak it out loud. Also several times if you want it.

Now the 2-Point-Method from quantum healing is used: put a hand on the middle of your thorax or hold it a few inches above it in the energy field. Now focus your perception on the palm of this hand. Watch exactly what happens. How does the inner surface feel? Do you feel a tingling or a pulling? Does heat even develop? Don't interpret, just perceive. Then place the other hand on your stomach or on your solar plexus just above the belly button or hold this hand a few inches above it in the energy field. Calm and without cramping. Now also notice the palm of the second hand and observe exactly what happens again. Do you feel a tingling, a pulling or warmth?

Now you always focus your perception alternately on the palm of the left hand and on the palm of the right hand. Finally, you perceive the two inner surfaces of your hands simultaneously, and ultimately with the same feeling. Do not seek advice from your rational mind, because it has just stopped anyway. Continue to observe what is happening and remain as an observer in perception. Enjoy the feeling of an all-encompassing tranquility. Not only do their hands feel the same, they are in sync with each other at this moment. Just like your left and right body halves. Your whole physical body adapts and is thereby brought into relaxation.

In the conventional way, the 2-Point-Method would be finished right now, but with the Brueckmann-Method it will be extended. But by other means.

You leave both hands where they are at the moment. However, the focus of the perception is now on your breathing, that is, you breathe in through the nose and out through the mouth again. Watch your breaths, which should still be calm and even. Now go into the imagination and imagine yourself as lively as possible as you create your perfectly identical light-twin with each new breath out of your spine. Your double resembles you in every detail like an egg to the other, only that your twin is transparent and bright, because it consists entirely of light. At first this light-figure is still small, but it grows with every breath to its full size. Throughout the journey through the adventure of your "fantasy world", your light-twin is always right behind you and looks over your shoulder at everything you experience. Further nothing. But he doesn't leave you like a good but silent friend. That would not be possible for him, because in your imagination you connect directly with him. At a specific point, your physical (already synchronized) body and your light-twin are coupled to each other, that is the location on the abdomen or solar plexus. In the imagination, you bind your light body to you, who is located directly behind you, so that you connect both points with a strongly luminous light beam: From the upper abdomen to the upper abdomen, a fixed light connection is created in this way, which is maintained during the coaching. Your physical body and your light body form a unit during the entire interactive experience. The fact that your light-twin takes a close look at you does not have to disturb you further. After all, he won't bother you either. He won't comment on anything or criticize anything.

Now you, along with your twin, are ready to go on the inner journey and can put your hands on your thighs. Be open to everything that can happen.

The adventure begins in the "fantasy world" you chose. As a coach, I will guide you into the respective initial situation and ask you to describe your observations and experiences very accurately during the course of the coaching. For example, what your surroundings look like, how your emotion changes, or what actions are taking place in your "fantasy world". Or who exactly you meet on your way. What are the encounters? (And of course this does not mean the light-twin.) Maybe you need to defend yourself or deliver something very important to someone?

Of course, I, as a coach, do not know what you are going to experience. Although the stories provide a fixed framework, they are as individual as the users or clients who consciously live inside these stories. Even if the outer form is the same, its content is always new. What is always prescribed is an "experiential way" from A to B. Most of the time, you are on foot in your imagination, but sometimes also sitting, although not all the time. For example, in a spaceship. (Your physical body sits upright in an armchair, on a sofa or on a bed.)

Eventually during the coaching you really merge with your story and are part of your fantasy world. The initial relaxation becomes pure excitement and desire for thrilling adventures. Meditation becomes interaction. You can rest when you go to sleep. With the Brueckmann-Method instead, your entire effort is required, at least in your imagination.

Sometimes I also remind you of the nose-mouth breathing and of maintaining the light connection between you and your light-twin in your imagination. And that you do not lose sight of your intention and goal.

Towards the end of every fantasy trip, you will receive an encrypted message that is intended only for you, that means, only you can decrypt this message. No one else. This can be in a very private letter, as a refractory message of a dragon, on the surface of a magical mirror, in a golden fruit of knowledge, as a holography, in a secret document or on the water surface of a wishing fountain.

The experiences in all "seven fantasy worlds" end in the same way: in order to decipher the encrypted message, it is necessary that you now connect the hearts of your physical body and your light body in your imagination, with a strong and bright light bridge. With your endeavour to decipher the message you have delivered or shown, you are now moving onto this radiant light bridge directly between your "two hearts". In attentive perception on the bridge you follow the conscious path into the inner heart of your light-twin: Around you on the bridge it becomes ever more pleasant and ever brighter until you have finally arrived inside your light heart. There you will find the answer to your question, the solution to your problem or the necessary hint to understand the message. Take your time.

When the right moment has come, we finish the coaching together. This moment is your decision alone. You leave the inner heart of your twin via the light bridge and thank your double for the help. Yes, you are filled with gratitude. You separate the connection to your light-twin from heart to heart and from belly to belly, so that your bright double can dissolve easily. Then you leave the "fantasy world" you chose and gradually return to your everyday life.

In exceptional cases, it may be experience that this answer, solution or notice is not immediately available, but does not appear internally or externally until a certain time after the coaching. It can also happen that a single session is not enough to receive the desired result.

Summary "The method in practice":

- one of "seven fantasy worlds" is selected, intention and goal are clearly formulated, notes for the security and to the surroundings are considered, you are prepared for physical reactions
- The coaching happens on the phone.
- Trust your imagination, your intuition and the higher consciousness.
- Show to the rational mind if necessary the red card. (criticism and doubt fade out)
- you use the 2-Point Method, with conscious breathing you create your "light-twin", connection with a bright beam of light from upper abdomen to upper abdomen
- The coach accompanies you mentally inside your fantasy world and puts questions to your interactive experiences.
- By the end you receive a coded message which only you can decipher namely in the "internal heart" of your "light-twin" (imagination: light bridge to the heart).
- You are filled with gratitude.

Check the result

Whether the decrypted message, answer or solution is correct for you or not, of course, only you can know. At the same time you feel it inside yourself, the result feels like it has torn down a wall, a wave of relief and joy comes over you. The blockade is gone and perhaps in the near future even a completely new phase of life begins in such a positive quality as has never been the case before.

If doubts arise in you, your rational mind will definitely speak. This could lead to the feeling that a few, but stubbornly disturbing remnants of the blockade have survived the process. Then you are not fully in resonance with your goal. In fact, if you are not sure whether you have finally redeemed your statement of intent, there is a very simple possibility of verification.

The very proven "window technology" is meant.

Application: After the end of your "fantasy journey", you are still energetically interacting with a higher level of consciousness. As if you had just enjoyed a full bath; the feeling of well-being continues for a while immediately after you have already climbed out of the tub.

In your real situation, you still sit upright and breathe evenly through your nose and through your mouth. So you go back to the initial position of the coaching and put your hands on the thorax and on the abdomen as before. Close your eyes and now imagine as clearly as possible that you sit – at eye level – directly next to a closed window. Don't think too much about it and get involved in it playfully.

You focus is on the result or the message you received at the end of the coaching session and you ask if the result is correct or wrong for you, either in silence or speaking aloud.

With the "energetically charged" hand in front of your thorax – because this area radiates the strongest energy from your body – try now in your imagination to gently open the window next to you. So you imagine pressing your "heart-hand" against the glass pane as if it were an action in your reality.

In a way, it is, too, because the test is equivalent to a kinesiological muscle test. The

Applied Kinesiology dates back to the 1960s and is due to the American chiropractor George Goodheart. The muscle tension gives a positive feedback and not the relaxation, as one might suppose.

Back to the "window technology": If the window remains closed and the window withstands the pressure, you can assume that the decrypted message, the received answer or the solution to your problem has been just right. This is tailored for you personally. So you can hold the force because the answer is true. The blockade has thus disappeared completely.

However, if you manage to open the window easily and without resistance in your imagination, then you press the glass pane outwards with your hand. This means that the energetic blockade has not yet completely resolved itself. Thus, the decoded message you have received is incomplete or full of gaps. In this case, you should simply wait for the next hours or days, whether the missing information is "delivered" to you internally or externally – usually very unexpectedly during everyday life. "Internally delivered" means that you suddenly come up with the solution. "Externally delivered" means that you get the solution through an external impulse. This can be, for example, a conversation, the headline of a newspaper, etc. If the answer remains, formulate a new, improved intention and goal to repeat the coaching using the Brueckmann-Method.

Meanwhile, it is important that you do not lie to yourself about the topic or situation you want to change positively. Of course, this is not always easy when it concerns things that have been part of the inner burdens for years that you would rather displace than really look at. Be brave. Because at some point you will realize that you have already left the hurdles behind you, because in the review they were actually no hurdles at all. Do not make yourself smaller than you are and never forget who you are in truth: a conscious creator.

Summary "Check the result":

- check the result which you have got at the end of your "fantasy trip", the "window technology" has proved itself
- You go back to the starting position of the coaching to the 2-Point Method.
- In your imagination you sit directly beside a closed window.
- Your focus is on the result and you ask for whether it is right for you or wrong.
- Now you try with the "heart hand" (chest) to push open the window softly: If the window pane stands firm to the pressure, the result is correct for you. If you succeed, however in opening the window pane without resistance, the result is not correct for you. (kinesiological muscle test). The energetic blockade is not completely solved yet.
- In the everyday life the missing information can be "delivered" later. If not, repeat the Brueckmann-Method with a new formulated declaration of intent.

The matrix

Now we look at the second big area of quantum physics, the quantum field theory. This non-material field of information is also called the "matrix". The word has different meanings. Two examples: In mathematics the matrix is an arrangement in table form, in the biology, however, it is the substance or the fabric portion between the cells (extra-cellular matrix). The word comes from the Latin language: "matricis" means "womb" and this is very exciting.

The term "the matrix" has become very popular since the American science fiction action movie of the same name with Keanu Reeves in the title role of the hacker "Neo" from 1999.

Also starring Laurence Fishburne, Carrie-Anne Moss and Hugo Weaving, directed by Lana and Lilly Wachowski, produced by Joel Silver, edited by Zach Staenberg., production companies: Warner Bros., Village Roadshow Pictures, Groucho II Film Partnership and Silver Pictures, distributed by Warner Bros.

In the film it is about artificial intelligence and virtual reality. "The Matrix" is shown as a green code within a grid net, consisting of different scriptures. Concerning the contents the film remains a very well made science fiction story, however, in his philosophy the film absolutely approaches to the field of information of the quantum field theory.

The information field consists – as the word says – of information. And these are simply present, ubiquitous. All possibilities of realities are stored and present in this field, so that the quantum mechanical "entanglement" also applies to quantum field theory and is effective in it. "The matrix" or "the quantum field" means an energy field. And energy is not lost, but is always transformed. Accordingly, everything is invisibly connected or networked. Everything is holographically "intertwined". The field lies outside of space and time and influences all living beings in their most diverse dimensional or consciousness levels within an energetic compression scale, which is not tangible with the mind because infinity does not occur in our imagination. In other words, "the matrix" could also be called "God" or "the universe" as another synonym for the highest consciousness.

By the way, scientifically measurable tests have shown that isolated DNA – the human genetic substance – can be emotionally influenced outside the body. Even if there is a separation of many kilometres between the dispenser and its sample.

In quantum physics, the quantum field theory goes far beyond quantum mechanics. The wave function is extended by the so-called "second quantization" in order – to say it in simple words – to capture not only one or some, but very many particles mathematically in their quantum physical behavior in realtion to different fields. It is about "multi-particle systems" in highly complicated calculations. Ever higher computing powers are necessary for this.

In Einstein's theory of relativity, the speed of light – about 300,000 kilometers per second – is the highest limit of the possible speed within space. This is traversed, for example, by a particle from A to B and the duration of the traversal is measured or calculated. But what happens if the calculation is not possible, not because the theory of relativity presupposes a vacuum, but because the passage of space did not take place at all despite the presence of the particle at goal B? Or the particle was even faster than the speed of light? (headword "tachyons")

This denotes again quantum-physical phenomena which are scientifically proved.

Albert Einstein got the Nobel prize for physics in 1921, by the way, not for the theory of relativity, but for the explanation of the "photoelectric effect", a further development after the quantum-physical presentation of Max Planck (light waves behave like particles).

In particle physics the quantum field theory and the theory of relativity are brought only partially in harmony, although the physical basic research aims at a complete union to come to a "Theory of Everything". Nevertheless, this can happen only under inclusion of the consciousness.

In a physical field – and also in the movie "The

Matrix" – it is about a force effect. Consciousness is not affected of it. It HAS no impacts of whatever kind. It IS. Fullstop.

If, however, one assumes that a force influence is chosen as a possibility of reality and thus becomes reality only through the observation of the observer, quantum physics can also be explained holistically.

The conscious focus of perception is, so to say, the "womb" of our reality. All the information that is imaginable is inside the matrix. The question remains whether they have always been there in principle, or whether the information does not arise until it is reactivated or caused by consciousness. In the first case our lives would be completely predestined, in the second case we would be the creators of our own destiny.

In my view, the alignment with the matrix and thus with an energetically highly effective quantum field is just another description of getting into the state or situation of a higher consciousness in order to obtain information that has a positive effect on one's way of life.

For sure, we as humans are not "trapped" in an

invisible information network, which foreshadows a virtual and controlled world, just as it is told in the film "The Matrix". And certainly we don't have to get rid of it. We should first recognize this as a compression of energy, and then make it usable for us.

Summary "The matrix":

- The energetic matrix or the quantum field is shown as a field of information in which all possibilities of realities exist which the consciousness can choose to create reality.
- Everything is invisible connected with everything and is holographically interwoven with each other.
- The field is outside from time and space and influences all living beings in her different dimension levels of the energetic compression.
- "the matrix" as a synonym for the highest, divine consciousness
- In the quantum field theory it is about the calculation of many particles systems.
- The speed of light as the uppermost border of the possible speed is doubtful.
- The physical aspiration to a "Theory of Everything" can succeed only under inclusion of the consciousness.
- The deliberate focus of the perception is the "womb" of our reality.
- the matrix as an energy compression

In the here and now

Imagination and creativity are alwasy outside of fixed time structures. The actions of children are based on this principle: therefore, we should learn again how to be like children. Children are free and carefree and can simply dedicate themselves to time. In the case of an adult who constantly and unconsciously converts the presumed "seriousness of life" into his reality, the opposite has happened: time does not only accompany his life, it determines his whole existence. The time for imagination and inspiration is missing. An adult usually swims against time and has forgotten not only to awaken his own imagination, but above all to devote and entrust himself to it.

Children are absolutely in the here and now, outside of past and future. They have completely forgotten the time around them and are in an infinite presence that has no beginning and no end. This present is only in the here and now. This means being completely with the I AM in the present.

It may sound abstract, but you can train yourself to fully engage in activities with all your senses, even in everyday life. An example that everyone knows: washing hair. What color is your shampoo? How do your hair feel when wet? How do you feel when you distribute the shampoo in it? What consistency does the foam form? What do you feel when the hair is finally dried and newly coiffed? And so on. Don't even think about it or analyze it in every detail, but just feel it and perceive it. Enjoy the moment. The rational mind remains outside.

Unfortunately, there are many people who have never learned to enjoy life – and thus never arrive in the present, that is, they make everything half-hearted or are constantly in the future with the thoughts, suspected worries and problems. Such people not only miss life, in the end they are missing themselves and the possible times of positive development. The result is either bitterness, resignation or disease.

Living in the here and now also means being in the right place in the right time. This cannot be planned, but is a result of intuition, of the "gut feeling".

One should always bear in mind that past and future are illusions. The past is already over and the future that so many people are afraid of has not yet happened. It's just an idea, a guess of what a situation might be like. Further nothing. So those who often go in thoughts into the past or into the future, prevent an active life in the present, in the here and now. This is the only time that life takes place. One cannot live before or later, only at this moment.

Even regretting a wrong decision in the past does not help anyone.

But what do you do if you feel so bad that you can't stand the here and now? Quite simply and often quite difficult at the same time: you fully accept the situation. Often it is only a judgment of the rational mind. If you do not accept the situation, you will quickly become the victim of your negative feelings. It is important to recognize you HAVE this or that negative feeling, you ARE not this or that feeling.

The situation can change quickly with

optimism, confidence or humor. Not by constant pondering. Once you can laugh at something, it has lost its negativity very reliably.

Trust yourself and your "inner voice" or your "gut feeling", your intuition, inspiration and imagination. Then you are back in trust to the present, in trust to the here and now. Be an active part of creation and thus of your own life. Have much fun and joy!

Summary "In the here and now":

- Most adults have forgotten in contrast to children how to be in here and now.
- not enough time for inspiration
- "In the here and now" means the infinite present of the I AM without time.
- The here and now can also be experienced in the everyday life with conscious and enjoyable perception outside the rational mind.
- With constant worry and fear about the future, people swear to have problems that don't even exist. Also, regretting a wrong decision in the past does not help anyone.
- Life is possible only in the here and now, one cannot live before or after.
- Accept also every negative feeling. Remain in the optimism, in the confidence and in the humor.
- Trust your intuition, inspiration and imagination, then you trust yourselves and your present in the here and now.
- Be an active part of the creation.

Book recommendations

Gregg Braden, "The Divine Matrix", Original English Language Publication 2007 by Hay House, Inc. California, USA

Gregg Braden, "The Spontaneous Healing of Belief", Original English Language Publication 2008 by Hay House, Inc. California, USA

Dr. Frank Kinslow, "The Secret of Instant Healing", 2008 by Lucid Sea, LLC.

Lynne McTaggart, "The Field", 2001 by HarperCollins Publishers, London

Eckhart Tolle, "The Power of Now – A Guide To Spiritual Enlightenment", 1997 by Namaste Publishing Inc. Vancouver, Canada, British Columbia, V6J1Z1

Jiddu Krishnamurti, "Freedom from the Known", 1973 by Krishnamurti Foundation Trust Ltd., Brockwood Park, Bramdean, Hampshire So24 0LQ England

Rhonda Byrne, "The Power", 2010 by Arria Books. A Division of Simon & Schuster, Inc., New York

Erich Fromm, "To Have or to Be?", 1976 by Harper & Row. Publishers, New York

Masaru Emoto, "Water is tell us precious things", 2001 by IHM, Tokio, Japan

Satprem, "Sri Aurobindo ou l'Aventure de la Conscience", 1970, Éditions Buchet / Chastel, Paris

About the author

Udo Brückmann, born 1967, lives as a mental coach, writer and teacher for German language in Lower Saxony, in the north of Germany. After graduating from high school relocation to Berlin in the divided city 1987, university studies of philosophy and history of art, various activities for stage, film and television (Deutsche Oper Berlin, Studio Babelsberg etc). Training as a city guide in Potsdam, education in scenic writing and screenwriting. Home care of the seriously ill parents; those were the most important years for learning about life. Later pedagogical training for inclusion and integration, teaching German language for refugees from war zones plus psychological care. Journalistic experiences, cosmopolitan, traveling around the world, confrontation with quantum physics and spirituality since three decades, coaching according to the Brueckmann-Method are part of it as a universal connection between physical and spiritual world. Personal note: It all began when I was a child with the fact, that

I noticed in elementary school that I can perceive the human aura brightly.

Work as published author: detective novels, historical novel, fantasy and fairy tales, short stories and poetry.

In 2011 the "Kindergedichte"/ "Children's Poems" were published after the NDR in Hamburg (German broadcasting and television) set the "Holzwurm" poem for "Mikado — Radio for Children" to music. Numerous publications in magazines and anthologies for various publishers followed, especially short stories and poetry: Sternenblick Berlin, Burgenwelt Verlag Bremen, Wendpunkt Verlag Weiden, Art Skript Phantastik Verlag Salach and others. For the publisher Geest-Verlag Vechta the novels "Zirkus Konzentrazani"/ "Circus Camponi" (together with Volker Hedemann about the background of the famous "Moorsoldatenlied", concentration camp Börgermoor 1933; also as unfilmed screenplay), "Ewig blüht das Leben"/ "Life blooms forever" (detective novel as a social satire on the subject of immortality, fictional background is the herbal medicine of Hildegard von Bingen as well as the alchemical spagyric according to Paracelsus) and "Mords-Hochschule - Bildung für alle"/ "Murder College – Education for Everyone" (detective novel as a satirical consideration of German pedagogy with a sociopolitical background) were created between 2013 and 2017. 2014 publication of the poems collection "Gedanken aus Licht"/ "Thoughts from Light" on the subject of spirituality and consciousness.

The partly new written "Mords-Hochschule" has had a second premiere in September 2019 as a funny stage reading together with German TV-Star Manon Straché. Since June 2019, a selection of "Children's Poems" has been set to music by the children's radio channel "KiRaKa" of the WDR in Cologne (Westdeutscher Rundfunk radio and broadcasting), since 2020 collaboration on the fairy tale project "BroOma" by Dutch-German actress and voice over artist Frauke Poolman, contributions for Youtube and several podcast providers.

You'll find detailed information about my person and about my work on my website: https://www.udo-brueckmann.de

Of course a summary description of the Brueckmann-Method as well as everything about the booking process is also to be read up there. Click on the subpage "Coachings".
On my website there is also a contact form which leads you directly to my service. In German and English.

As a coaching classic, there is an additional option on offer for everyone who wants to use their time much better and more effectively, this is TIME MANAGEMENT. Also for companies in the context of business consulting / management consultancies. The seven best methods are available: The Pareto principle, the Priority matrix, the ABC analysis, the Eisenhower principle, the ALPEN method, the SMART method as well as Kiss The Frog.

Reference: The quote from Max Planck on page 3 can be found on the website https://beruhmte-zitate.de/autoren/max-planck/

Note of thanks

Special thanks to Willehad Heyermann, Christa and Günter Unglaub, Silvia Stoll, Saskia Walentowitz, Dirk Nilsson, Dorothy Nesbit, Oliver Schell and to my family

The Brueckmann-Method
Tangible ways
in fantasy worlds

Coaching

...available also in German.